The Greatest Story Never Told

ISBN 978-1-0980-8892-7 (paperback)
ISBN 978-1-6387-4486-3 (hardcover)
ISBN 978-1-0980-8893-4 (digital)

Copyright © 2021 by Timothy J. Wright

All rights reserved. No part of this publication may be reproduced, distributed, or transmitted in any form or by any means, including photocopying, recording, or other electronic or mechanical methods without the prior written permission of the publisher. For permission requests, solicit the publisher via the address below.

Christian Faith Publishing, Inc.
832 Park Avenue
Meadville, PA 16335
www.christianfaithpublishing.com

baker@calvaryeagles.org

Printed in the United States of America

The Greatest Story Never Told

Timothy J. Wright

Illustration by Susan A. Baker

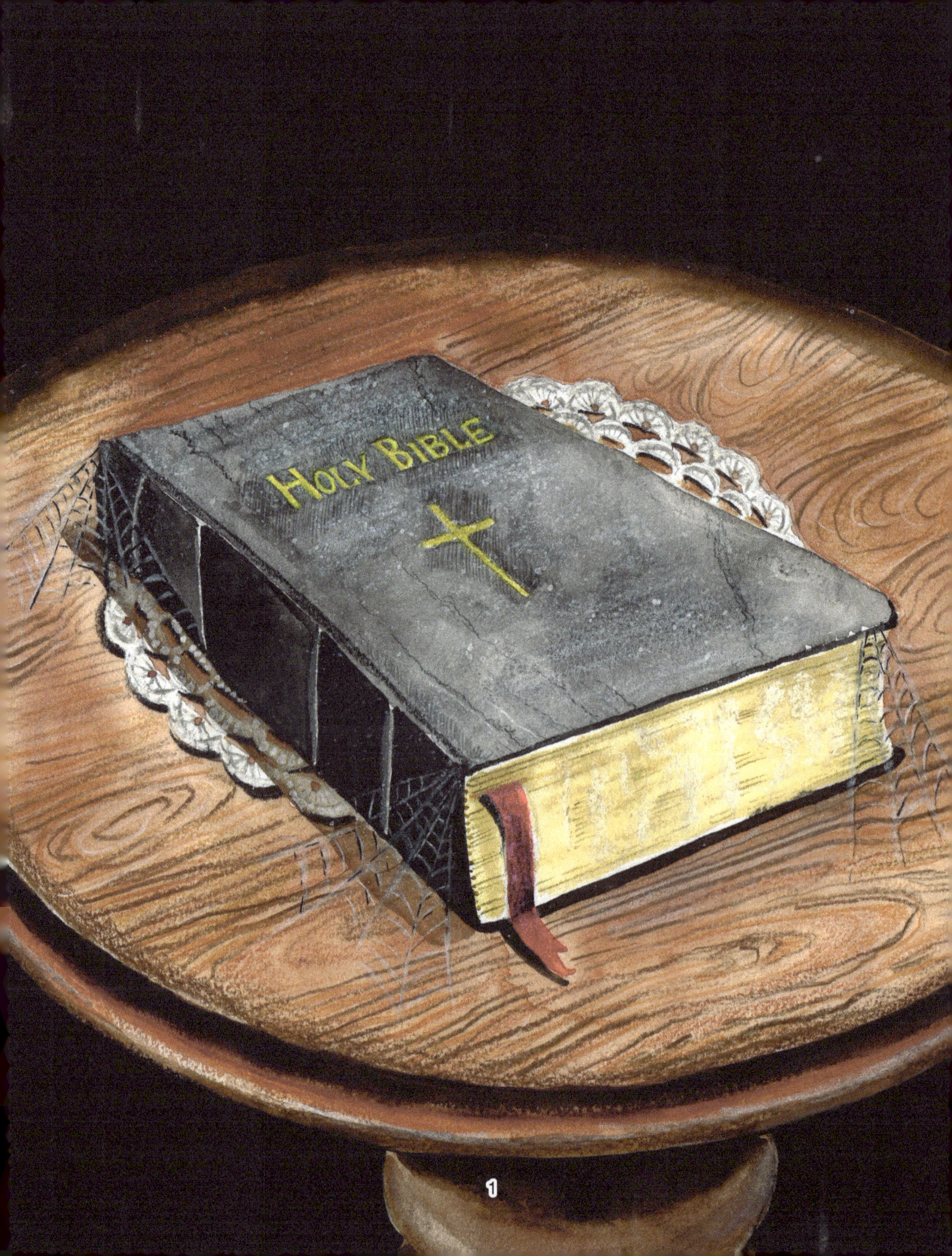
HOLY BIBLE

Chapter 1

The Greatest Story Never Told

Just imagine there's a God who created all you see.
And that He's a God of love, so He created you and me.
He wrote a book to tell his story so all creation could see his glory.
But then his children did something very hard to believe.
All the things that He created; they began to worship these.
And the Book that He gave them that told of all his glory.
They refused to believe it and made up a different story.

③

His creation screams out, "I'm a very big God!"
But his children took trees, and made their gods out of these.
They began to worship the god of their hands and soon forgot the
God who made them.

They built houses and boats and played with their games.
And said to themselves, "Nothing has changed."
Things that ever were and ever will be, they all stay the same.
It's just you and me.

So the greatest story of the God of old was hardly ever even told.
Yes, they forgot God, and when death knocks on their door,
they'll stand before the One they were created for.
Won't they be surprised, they thought He was dead.
Have you opened up your Bible to find out what God said?

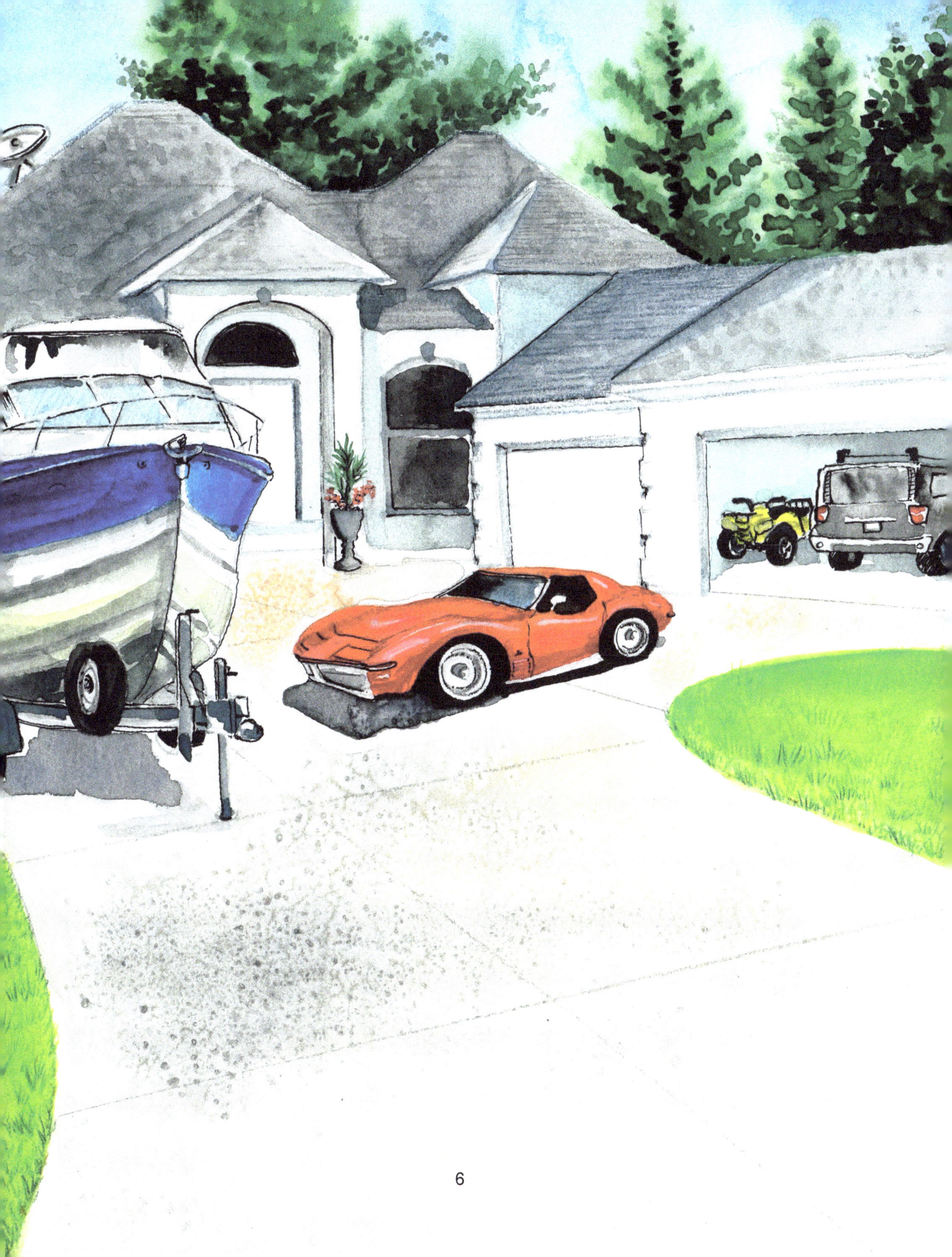

7

Chapter 2

The Greatest Story Ever Told

Let's tell the old-time story—we'll go back line by line.
Let's take it way back to the ancient of time.
Before the great mountains and before the great seas, in the heart of our father there was you there was me.
We must tell this story because there's a story to tell;
so why's there a heaven and why's there a hell?

It starts in a garden and ends on a tree—Oh Lord, give us ears, give us eyes we can see.

10

11

So let's tell the story.

13

There was a king who walked this land—
the messiah they did call him—the
word of God in the flesh of man. He spoke
of love and freedom to a world so
lost in sin, but his message burned like fire
in every heart that would let him in.

"I have many things I need to tell you—
my time down here is almost
through, but when I'm gone, you will remember
all these things I've said to you.
Right now you're sad because I leave you;
but if I go, I'll come again.
Don't let the enemy deceive you—I give you power over him.

16

17

I saw him falling from the skies; and now my church, it will arise.
I go to conquer death and sin—then I will be with you again.
You say where will you go because we will
follow—but where I go you cannot be.
I am returning to the Father—now you must learn to trust in me.
In a little while you'll all forsake me; the
Prince of Darkness comes for me.
But don't forget the words I've told you,
"I make myself an offering.""

Now as they watched him bleed and suffer, here's where He proved his love for you when he cried out, "Father, forgive them, they know not what they do."

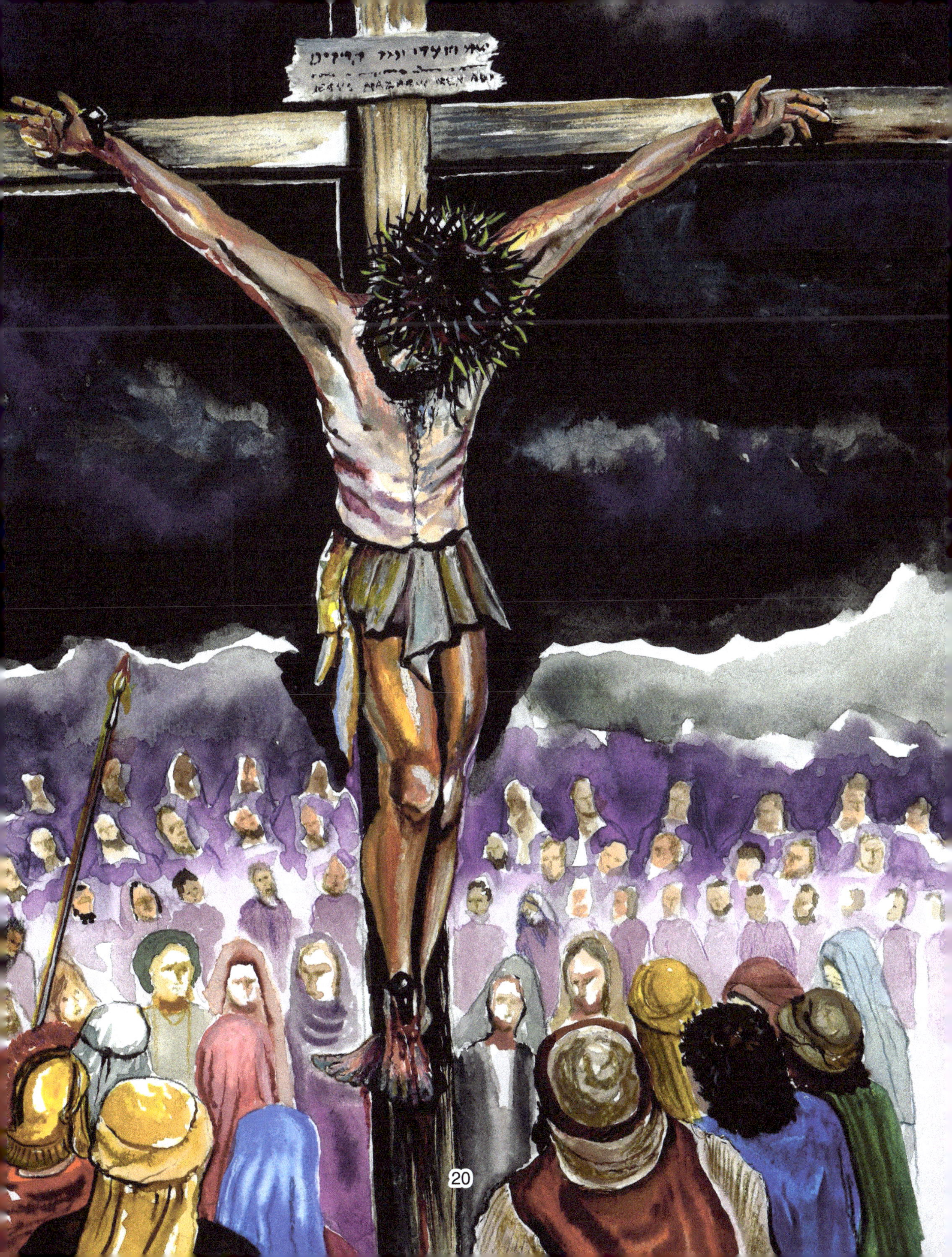

21

This story might have ended and maybe never
told again, but on the third day
he had risen—yes, he was risen from the dead.
And now his glory reigns in heaven, but his spirit's on this land.
And to this day, his name is precious; he
set us free—all praise to Him.
It pleased the Lord what he had done; the prophets tell us so,
because in his heart was you and me—that cross is where he'd go.

The Father took him home again and sat him on his throne,
but He had written the greatest story the world has ever known.
The people began to doubt and say, "Is this what God has done?"
But all the demons shook with fear; they knew he was the one.

24

25

We heard a cry before God's throne from
those who had been slain.
"How long, oh, Lord, before you come—before you take us home?"
"A little while," we heard him say, "and the earth will be my throne."

The seals were opened one by one, God's judgment
had begun. No peace just death and war and
pain; the demons thought they'd won.
At last, we heard a trumpet sound, and it
was time to go. We were right there
by his side. When He drew his sword, the people cried.

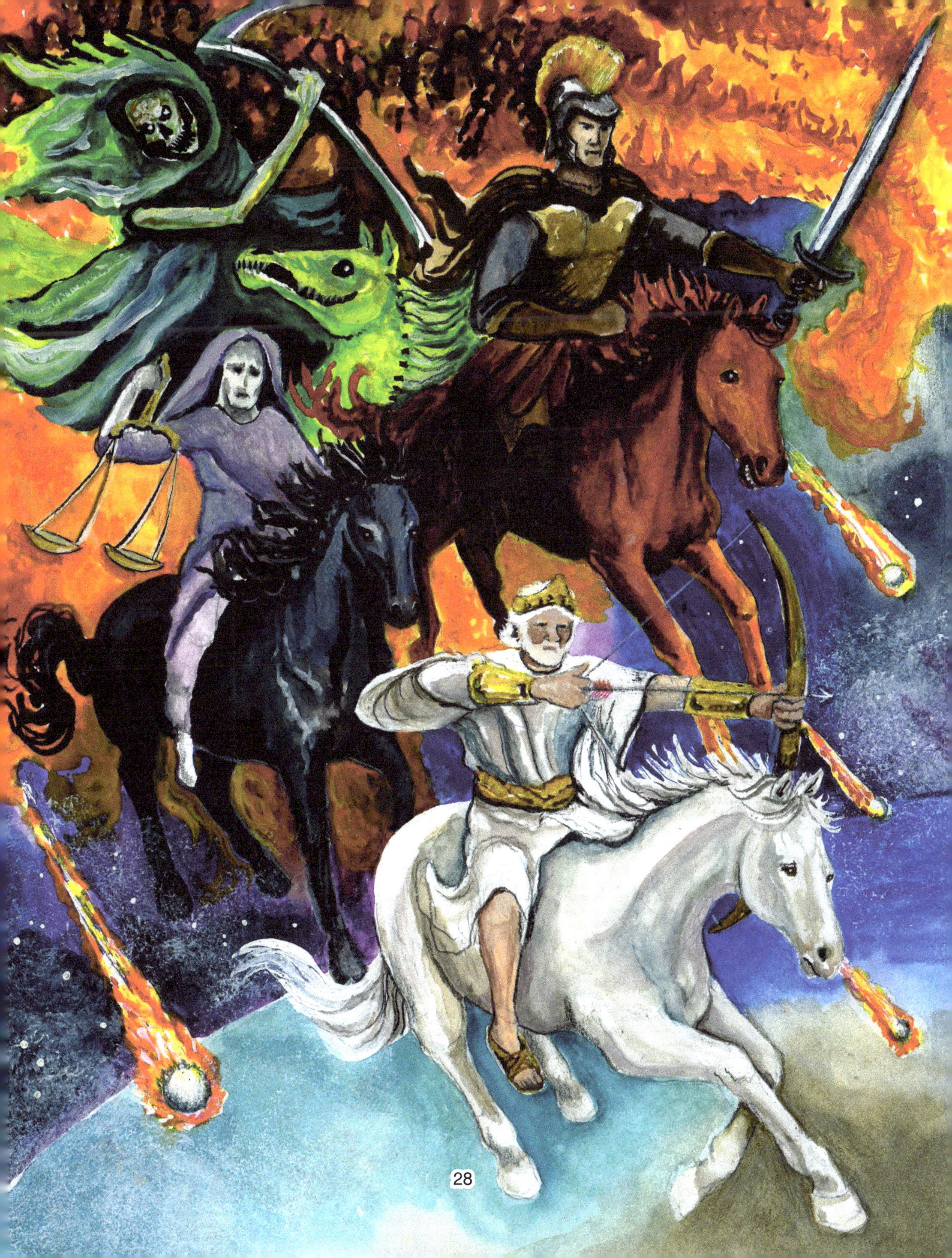

29

"The battle is the Lord's." He spoke one
word, and it was through his victory
sure and fast. When victory came, creation sang,
"Oh death, oh death, where is your sting?"
Then all the world began to sing, "We've
been redeemed, we've been
redeemed!"

God's promise kept his word was true—death and sin would no
more rule. Jesus is the Lamb of God, and now he's Lord of all.
One day we'll rule and reign with him—
come on, don't miss his call.
Just imagine you're NOT in Heaven because
Jesus Christ was not your Lord.
In your life, you did it your way; you tried
Him once, but you were bored.
Many times God tried to call you, but in
your heart you turned away.
Friends and loved ones tried to warn you; "That works for you" is
what you'd say.
Now your life on earth has ended; every chance you had is gone.
You stand before him empty handed and
realize that you were wrong.

32

Right now there's hope because you're still
living; one more chance you
get today. God's calling everyone to serve
him; most will turn and walk away.
You could delete or trash this message,
or you could rise up to his call.
Become a warrior in God's army then
stand before him proud and tall.
I hope we all get to heaven, but God's Word is very clear.
That most will miss by eighteen inches—
between their heart and their ear.
Oh, I know they'll say we're hypocrites and
guess what—it's probably true.
But we found grace, and we found mercy—I
pray to God you find it too.
And are we really hypocrites? Now you could make the case.
Because we mess up and now and then—
we're known to make mistakes.
But when we fall down, we get up again.
We learn; we grow; we follow him.
It's what you don't know I really fear. Because
our eyes can see and our ears
can hear.

I don't know how, but I remember when I
prayed the sinner's prayer to him.
So, God, to you my prayer will be—you'll
open their eyes so they can see.
Now if you want you can pray with me,
"Lord Jesus, I've sinned, and I've lost
my way. I forgot your cross and the price
you paid. I have nothing to offer
and nothing to give; I cry out for your
mercy and my sins to forgive."
Now if you really meant that prayer, there's
a party in heaven with angels
there. They're singing and dancing around
God's throne because one more
child of his came home.
But there's one more thing that you must do
to seal your faith and prove it's true—
go tell someone what God has done.
You once were blind but now you see. You don't know how, but
you remember when—you prayed a sinner's prayer to him.

Chapter 3

The Lion and the Seven Seals

Come with me to a place where imagination
and reality tell a story.
In a time when people are living for today
and not thinking about tomorrow,
it's good to remind ourselves how important
our past is to our future.
Let's take a glimpse of what might have
been happening in heaven as our
past was unfolding then bring us into today, and use God's word
to tell the story of tomorrow. With The
Lion And The Seven Seals.

The First Seal Was Opened

My son, you must go quickly. The false church is spreading lies.
Your seed is being threatened…and I have heard their cries.
The Lion roared as He left the throne…
His speed was faster than light.
Satan was trying to destroy His seed…
now the Lion would need to fight.

First, he would take a remnant to a place across the sea.
And bring them to an unknown land…far from their enemy.
The people laughed as they boarded ships…
"You'll fall off the edge of the earth."
But the lion would lead them to a new land,
and America would find her birth.
The times were hard…the winters long, but
they would finally have a home.
The Lion would not leave their side till
His seed could stand alone.
Satan's anger was being unleashed to all who opposed his lie.
The blood of the martyrs would plant the
seeds, the false church begins to die.

Filled with fury and filled with rage, he would go to the new land.
In his revenge, attack God's seed and try to rule over them.

But the Lion stirred the people, and when
they prayed through the night.
Those farmers went out as warriors, but not in their own might.
This army was strong and well prepared,
but the people continued to pray.
Those farmers took their pitchforks and
mowed them down like hay.
The Lion's roar shook the earth…it was a roar of victory.
The people shouted, "Our God reigns!" as
they watched their enemy flee.

The Second Seal Was Opened

Son of man speak to these bones…they must live again.
They are the apple of my eye, but they are dead because of sin,
I must bring them back from the east and from the west,
They have wandered many years…now I will give them rest.

Then I heard the Lion roar, and the bones came together again.
He breathed in them the breath of life, and
they marched toward Jerusalem.
This was a people so despised…many years they would roam.
But they were precious in the Father's eyes,
and now they're going home.

The people cried, "It isn't fair, they don't deserve this land."
So they gathered together all the armies from
the north to go make war with them.
Overwhelmed by fear…now what would Israel do?
Then I heard the Lion say…"I will prove I have loved you."

The earth began to shake…the sky turned black as night.
The Lion roared the battle's won… Israel didn't even fight.
Then they looked on Him who they had pierced, their
eyes were filled with tears. The Lion of Judah, You were
the one…we've been blind for all of these years.

"Jerusalem, Jerusalem…even though you went astray. Many
years have come and gone… I have waited for this day."
Then the Lion began to weep, like a father weeping for his only
son. "Bring them home I heard Him say…bring them everyone."
He wept so loud, it shook the earth…all the demons ran below.
The nations trembled when they heard His
cry saying, "Let my people go."

The Third Seal Was Opened

The Lion's on the move…people are beginning to seek His face.
We hear of wars and rumors of wars…
this world's becoming a scary place
Could this be the last harvest… I know
we won't know when or how,
But one thing is for sure…the Lion's on the prowl.

He's the Lion of Judah… He puts the nations in their place.
They are right where He predicted…
the time is short if that's the case.
If you're not careful, you could miss Him
as you go about your merry way.
The signs are really all around us…
this is a time to watch and pray.

When the Lion strikes, it will be deadly…
He's calling warriors to march with Him.
The last battle will be for us… He's going
to break the power of sin.
Only a remnant will He use…choose the side you will be on.
Because when the trumpet makes a sound,
don't look for us…we will be gone.

Then our Lord will appear with vengeance in His eye
He's not the helpless Lamb of God…
now He's the ferocious El Shadi!
Every mountain will be leveled when the King is on His throne.
Only He is lifted up, for He is God and God alone.

Today's the day to get ready…tomorrow belongs just to Him.
This could be your last chance before the Lion strikes again.

The Forth Seal Was Opened

The weak are yelling out, "Look at me—I
am strong!" They now have the
secrets to the nuclear bomb. The nations
are fearful—will it get any worse?
As they test their new bombs and continue
to curse. The people want peace
now, and at any price, did they just open
the door for the antichrist?
Seven years of tribulation—did it all just
begin? God's people are wondering—
Could this be the end? A leader emerges but not in his own power.
He claims he is God—this is his hour. He
says he'll bring peace throughout all
the land. And that he's their messiah—the world worships him.
He curses God's laws—all power is mine. And
an unholy trinity begins to unwind.
He makes war with the saints—they have no
power over him. If the church has
been raptured, one by one they join them.

But now, he has trouble coming
out of the East. These nations won't
submit to his new plans of peace.
So, greedy for power, he has a new plan, He'll
go to Jerusalem and make peace
with them.

When the peace treaties signed, God's people all know there's
three and a half years of suffering to go. He
defiles the temple just like Daniel
foretold—the abomination of desolation that was spoken of old.
It's the time of Jacob's trouble, there could
be no doubt. God's people all hide
to wait this thing out. Now the judgments
of God all start to begin—Satan
knows that his time will come to an end.

"Worship me," he demands—"because your
God is dead." Those that don't
worship will all lose their head.
I wish I could tell you this story's not true,
and America will always be free.
But half of this story has already happened—the rest is yet to be.

The Fifth Seal Was Opened

The fullness of the gentiles was finally now all in.
His thousand-year reign was just starting to begin.
The line to see the Lion stretched out for miles.
The first in line were those in life who had the hardest trials.

"But who are these all dressed in white?" I heard an angel say.
They were those who fought the beast
that the antichrist would slay.
They shined like the morning sun, and
a new name was given them.
The Lion called them "faithful" because
they were faithful to the end.

You could always find them very near to the throne.
The Lion made them pillars in the temple of his home.
These were those who fought their flesh, even on to death.
Some in line were grieved when they saw their faithfulness.

And others were very sad because they did not give their all.
In life they were too selfish and missed God's higher call.
They wished they could go back if only for one day.
And do the things they should have done,
but time had slipped away.
We will all give an account one day of what we did or did not do.
Aren't you glad it's not too late for me and for you?
So remember now when life gets tough…be faithful through it all;
And you could be a pillar in God's temple standing tall.

The Sixth Seal Was Opened

The Book of Life was opened…this was not the place to be.
If your name wasn't found in the Book of
Life, you were damned for eternity.
This is the Great White Throne Judgment,
and at His feet you will fall.
Every tongue will confess and proclaim that He is Lord of all.

It is appointed to us once to die…
then the judgment, good or bad.
No one can pray you in or out…that was a lie that Satan had.
There's no in between place…it's only Heaven or hell.
And no such place called purgatory…that was another lie as well.

If living your life in paradise is just not for you, there's really
only one more choice…so choose between the two.
One thing I must warn you now in case you didn't know,
you might think God is rather mean…it really isn't so.

Those who went to hell fought God's love every day because all creation shouts His glory, but they refuse to pray. Being a nice person will never get you in. Satan thinks he's also nice, so you'll end up with him. God so loved the world that He gave His only Son. So don't forget it's heaven or hell…you need to choose which one. Don't be like the ostrich and stick your head in the sand. Look up and see there is a God and begin to worship Him. I hope you heed this warning if Heaven is not your home. You'd be better off eaten by a great white shark than end up at the Great White Throne.

Seventh Seal Was Opened

There's more to life than what our eyes can see; and there's
more to God than what our dreams could ever dream.
One day you could wake up and be walking on streets of gold;
and up ahead you'll see a crystal sea around God's royal throne.
Now I'm not talking about Disneyland
or a place called *make believe*.
I'm talking about God's house—it's way
bigger than you ever dreamed!
It's 1,500 miles square and it's coming down from the sky, and
even though it is so big, you could miss it when you die.

Now I don't claim to have been there or to
have walked the streets of gold.
But the One who tells the story—He's the builder, I am told.
The walls are made of jasper—it's beyond your wildest dream.
This is not some ordinary house—this is a palace for the King.
God gave the vision in Revelation—to John he would not
hide; it was dazzling white so beautiful looking like a bride.

When you enter into this house, there is no need for light.
No sun or moon will shine in it—God's glory is so bright!
This is more like a city—it has three gates on each side.
And each gate has one pearl—so big it could open wide.
But there was one more thing that John
did see; and this one thing really
bothered me.
There were lots of loved ones that did not make it there,
but God himself was wiping away everybody's tears.
Heaven's not a fairy tale—every word of God is
true. But when your loved ones get to heaven,
will God be wiping their tears for you?

About the Author

I went to school in the seventies, and school was something I just wanted to be over with. I'm sure back then they had no clue what dyslexia was, at least not at my school. To me, school was terrifying, especially English. What if the teacher would call on me to read out loud or to spell something? By the time I got to high school, I would be in special reading classes. I flunked English twice and was told I would not graduate with my graduating class. But after my mom gave the principal a piece of her mind and told him I had been on the honor roll the year before when I did not have to take English, he would let me graduate with my class.

For over thirty years, I would have dreams that I was still in high school trying to get my diploma. I have a good friend who had read my books and who asked me if I had taken advanced English classes in high school! I just laughed as I told him my story and still do today just thinking about it. I always wondered why it was so hard for me to do certain things that other kids seemed to do so easily.

When I gave my heart to Jesus, I would begin to understand why. Over and over again after I got saved, He would keep showing me how that in my weakness His strength is made perfect. I am not saying this for my glory, but He has helped me write eight books, lead a prison ministry for over twenty years, and speak at a local men's rescue mission—all things that used to terrify me before. But even now I cannot do these things without saying those words, "Lord, in my weakness will You be my strength." Yes, God took the weakest thing that I ever had and said, "I can use that." To Him be always the glory and honor and power forever. Amen.

CPSIA information can be obtained
at www.ICGtesting.com
Printed in the USA
LVHW070839040921
696886LV00005B/3

9 781638 744863